MW01593839

The Reward Of Confidence

By Charles Cowan

CHARLES COWAN
PUBLICATIONS

Unless otherwise indicated, all Scripture quotations are taken from the *King James Version of the Bible*.

The Reward of Confidence
ISBN 0-943109-02-7
Second Edition
Copyright © 2003 by Charles Cowan
Charles Cowan Publications
P. O. Box 160268
3344 Walton Lane
Nashville, TN 37216

Editorial Consultant: Cynthia Hansen
Book Design: CBS Music City Printing / Carole Davis

Table of Contents

Introduction

Prayer of Salvation

Introduction

We are about to take a little different approach to the book of Hebrews than you may have done in the past.

What do I mean by that? Well, you are probably aware that throughout the book of Hebrews, the apostle Paul talks about the New Covenant and explains why it is a better covenant than the old one. He goes to great lengths to explain why the sacrifice of Jesus was a better sacrifice than the animal sacrifices that the Israelites offered to the Lord in the wilderness.

If you have studied the Old Covenant, you also know that God made its provisions available to every individual who would adhere to the commandments contained within that covenant. As long as God's people kept the covenant, they wouldn't have a need. They could always obtain healing from any sickness or disease that might attack their bodies. They could obtain deliverance from every problem or crisis that confronted them. However, they had to obey the covenant principles by doing what God told them to do in order for them to receive any of the benefits God had provided through that covenant.

Paul spends a great deal of time in Hebrews talking about what is available to us as Christians today under the New Covenant — the better covenant. He first tells us that, under the Old Covenant, the high priest had to atone for his own sins before he was allowed to go into the Holy of Holies and offer sacrifices for his people. Then Paul tells us about Jesus — the sinless, spotless, perfect Lamb of God.

We don't have to offer animal sacrifices any longer to atone for our sins because Jesus offered His own blood for us once and for all. Jesus entered into the heavenly Holy of Holies to present His holy blood in the Presence of Almighty God — not to atone for sins He had committed, but for the sins of all people.

It is our faith and trust in the blood of Jesus that cleanses us from all sin. How much better is that precious blood than the blood of a goat or a bullock!

For so long, we have looked at the book of Hebrews as the great book on redemption by blood — and praise God, it is definitely that! But Hebrews has many other important truths to teach us if we will just take the time to study it.

We're going to explore one of those important truths in the following pages. My purpose in writing this book is to enable you to discover the reward of confidence as presented in the book of Hebrews. I want you to personally apply these principles to your own life so you can reap that reward on a daily basis.

So read these words carefully. Search the Word of God to make sure what I am sharing with you is truth. As you allow the Holy Spirit to become your Teacher and begin to apply these truths to your daily walk with Christ, you will find yourself enjoying the reward of confidence — a more abundant life than you ever imagined possible!

Charles Cowan

Chapter 1
Confidence:
Your Confession of Faith

Cast not away therefore your confidence, which hath great recompence of reward.

Hebrews 10:35

At one time or another, you have probably said these words: "I sure have confidence in that person. His word is his bond. If he tells you he will do something, he will do it." But what do you mean when you say that you have *confidence* in someone?

First, let's go to the dictionary to learn some different definitions of the word *confidence. Funk and Wagnalls Standard Desk Dictionary* gives us several meanings: "A feeling of trust in a person or thing; reliance; faith; self-assurance; fearlessness; a relationship of trustful intimacy."[1]

In the Greek, the word *confidence* means in essence *free outspokenness about what you are saying*. In other words, your *confidence* is synonymous to your *confession of faith*.

---

[1] *Funk and Wagnalls Standard Desk Dictionary* (New York: Funk and Wagnalls, 1974).

So what are you saying? Are you saying, "Oh, my, things are so bad. If they get any worse, I'm just going somewhere to hibernate"? If you are saying words like these, you are *casting away your confidence*.

The Just Shall Live by Faith

Let's look at Hebrews 10:35 in context so we can better understand what the apostle Paul is saying:

For ye had compassion of me in my bonds, and took joyfully the spoiling of your goods, knowing in yourselves that ye have in heaven a better and an enduring substance.

Cast not away therefore your confidence, which hath great recompence of reward.

For ye have need of patience, that, after ye have done the will of God, ye might receive the promise.

For yet a little while, and he that shall come will come, and will not tarry.

Now the just shall live by faith: but if any man draw back, my soul shall have no pleasure in him.

But we are not of them who draw back unto perdition; but of them that believe to the saving of the soul.

Hebrews 10:34-39

Paul tells us in verse 38 that "...*the just shall live by faith*...." He doesn't say, "Maybe they'll live by faith." He doesn't say, "I hope so" or "I think so." He says, "The just *shall* live by faith."

You may ask, "But who *are* the just?" *The just* are those who have been redeemed by the blood of Jesus.

If we are Christians, we are "the just." However, we must live by faith. No matter how often we go to church or how many times we sing or testify, if we are not living by faith — the way God intends for us to live — we are not pleasing Him. Hebrews 11:6 says, *"But WITHOUT FAITH IT IS IMPOSSIBLE TO PLEASE HIM: for he that cometh to God must believe that he is, and that he is a rewarder of them that diligently seek him."*

What *Is* Faith?

Colossians 1:10 describes how you are to live as one of "the just": *"That ye might walk worthy of the Lord unto all pleasing, being fruitful in every good work, and increasing in the knowledge of God."* In order for you to walk in a manner worthy of and pleasing to the Lord, you are going to have to walk by faith —day by day, moment by moment, in every situation you face. But in order to *live by faith*, you have to know the meaning of *faith*.

Faith is acting on what the Word of God says, regardless of the circumstances, regardless of what you see with your physical eyes. You respond according to what the Word of God says about the situation you face, *not* according to the circumstances.

You may say, "But I don't feel like I have any faith."

Your feelings play no part in whether you do or don't have faith. If you have trusted Jesus as your Savior and Lord, you have been given the measure of faith (Rom. 12:3).

Paul was inspired to write, "*...without faith it is impossible to please him....*" Since God said you must walk by faith in order to please Him, it wouldn't be fair for Him to say, "You'll just have to get faith the best way you can." Thus, God gives you the measure of faith so you can live in a manner pleasing to Him. However, He then expects you to use the faith you've been given by acting on His Word in every situation.

How can you know if you (one of "the just") are living by faith? I'll tell you one easy way to find out — just listen to what you are saying. Check to see if you have cast away your confidence through words of doubt and unbelief.

For instance, if you are only saying, "I hope God will do this for me," then you are missing the substance of *faith*. Hope is like a dream. By itself, it has no substance nor tangibility.

When you have a dream at night, it seems real. It is almost as though you were there. But the moment you awaken, that dream is gone. The only tangible thing you have left is the bed in which you were sleeping when you had the dream.

Hope is like that dream. You are never able to put your hand on it until you add the substance of *faith*.

Hebrews 11:1 says that faith becomes the evidence, or proof, of things not seen with the physical eye. For instance, suppose you are believing God for your healing and you are in terrible pain. Your faith is the evidence of the healing you don't yet see with your physical eyes. Therefore, you must respond according to your faith if someone asks you, "How do you feel?"

If you tell the person how you feel, he will think you are not healed. But you can answer him this way: "Well, let me tell you what I believe. I believe that according to Isaiah 53:5, Jesus took my infirmities and bore my sicknesses, and I was healed. I believe God's Word; therefore, according to my faith, I believe I have received my healing." With your words, you have brought your faith into the *now* — present tense. Your faith is *proof* that you are healed, and your confession of faith demonstrates your *confidence* in God's faithfulness to perform His promises.

Your faith will bring your healing that is not yet seen into the natural realm where it will be visible to all. Then if someone asks you how you are feeling, you can answer, "I am feeling great! I am healed." But until then, your faith is based on what the Word of God says.

Faith always operates in the realm of the unseen. You don't have to have faith for something you need if you can already see it.

For instance, if you were standing next to me and I told you that I had a quarter in my hand, you wouldn't need any faith to accept that statement as true if you could see the quarter in my hand. But what if I stuck my hand in my pocket or put my hand behind my back and then said, "I have a quarter in my hand"? You would have to accept my word in order to believe me.

In the same way, you are going to have to determine that God would not lie to you for you to be able to believe and act upon His Word.

Does God ever lie? No! He first said in Isaiah 53:5, "*...and with his stripes we are healed.*" Many years later, Peter confirmed this eternal truth of redemption: *"Who his own self bare our sins in his own body on the tree, that we, being dead to sins, should live unto righteousness: by whose stripes ye were healed"* (1 Peter 2:24).

Notice that the phrase "were healed" is past tense. That's why you should never pray, "God, will You please heal me?" Peter said, "By His stripes you were healed." You *were* healed when the stripes were laid upon Jesus' back. Therefore, by faith you receive *now* what has already been done for you.

Faith is the evidence, or the substance, of the things you can't see. Faith is not the evidence of insubstantial hope. It is not the stuff of mere

11

fantasies or dreams. Faith is the evidence of things you have prayed for that will eventually become manifested in this natural realm. As Jesus said, *"Therefore I say unto you, What things soever ye desire, when ye pray, believe that ye receive them, and ye shall have them"* (Mark 11:24).

You may say, "Well, Brother Charles, I can't believe something I can't see."

But think about it — you believe things you can't see every day of your life. For instance, you believe that radio and television stations around the world are broadcasting right now. At this very moment, they are transmitting invisible signals through the atmosphere. You can't see those signals, but you believe they are there. Why? Because every time you turn on your television set or radio, the receiver picks up those signals and transforms them into either picture or sound.

Look at Mark 11:24 again. Notice that Jesus didn't say, "What things soever *God* desires for you." He said, "What things soever *you* desire, believe that you receive them when you pray." Jesus didn't say, "You have to *feel like* you receive them when you pray." He said, "*Believe* that you receive the things you desire when you pray." If you don't believe you receive your petition when you pray — and that is always in the present tense — you won't get anything.

If you believed you received when you prayed, you need not ask God for your petition again. If you pray for it a second time, you didn't believe you received it in the first place. In essence you are saying, "Well, Lord, I know I asked You for this before, but I just don't know for sure if I've received my answer yet. So I'm asking You for it again, just to make sure."

If you truly believed you received when you prayed, you would say, "Thank You, Father, for giving me the answer to my prayer. Thank You, Father. It is mine; I have it now. I see it with the eye of faith. My faith is the evidence or proof of that which I don't see. I have it now, and, Father, I thank You and praise You for it."

You see, praise is faith in action. Faith isn't head understanding; it is spiritual understanding from the heart. Therefore, you will save yourself a lot of wasted time if you'll establish this truth in your heart: *Faith is always present tense*. As Paul said in Hebrews 11:1, *"NOW faith is...."*

Ask According to God's Will

In First John 5:14,15, John wrote this: *"And this is the confidence that we have in him, that, if we ask any thing according to his will, he heareth us: And if we know that he hear us, whatsoever we ask, we know that we have the petitions that we desired of him."*

John did *not* say, "This is the confidence we have in God: if we *feel good* when we ask, He hears us." Thank God, our feelings have nothing to do with His willingness to hear and answer our prayers!

You may say, "Yes, but I don't know the will of the Lord." Well, that's a simple problem to fix. You will find the will of the Lord in His Word, so take the time to get into the Word of God. Determine to believe whatever God says about your situation; then find His will in His Word before you pray. If you don't, you are wasting your time. He only hears you as you ask according to His will.

At that point, your faith becomes the evidence of what you can't yet see. *Faith will stand in the gap* until the petition you have believed God for comes into manifestation. Until you can see it with your physical eyes, your faith is the proof that you have received it. In other words, faith is the *title deed* to what things soever you desire from God.

Suppose someone came to me and said, "Brother Charles, I just bought you a house and five acres of land. I'm giving it to you. Here is the *title deed* to it. It's legal."

I'd say, "Thank you." Then I'd tell everyone that I have a house. Even though I have never seen my house, I have the *title deed* to prove that I own it.

That's why it is impossible to please God without faith — the *title deed* that gives you the assurance that God's promises are yours. It is only as you walk by faith that you walk in a manner pleasing unto the Lord.

So no matter what happens or what circumstances you may face in life, hold fast to your confession of faith. *Cast not away your confidence — the free "outspokenness" of the faith in your heart that God's Word WILL come to pass in your life!*

Chapter 2
Take Joyfully
The Spoiling of Your Goods

As we study this passage in Hebrews 10, some of the truths presented may be foreign to your thinking. Some of the teachings gleaned from this passage of Scripture through the years may not even be what Paul was actually talking about.

For instance, Paul said that the Hebrews *took joyfully the spoiling of their goods* (Heb. 10:34). Apparently, these people who had shown compassion for Paul were being persecuted. Some of their material possessions had been spoiled by others. Students of the Bible know that a great persecution of the Church was going on at that time. Apparently, this was what Paul was referring to.

Think about it — suppose someone walked into your house, opened the refrigerator door, and threw all your food onto the floor. Then he went to the pantry and threw all its contents on the floor. Finally, he found the cookie jar where you had hidden all your savings, took out the money, and kept it for himself.

Would you take that person's actions joyfully? *No!* You'd probably be ready to fight. You would run that person out of your house, and if you couldn't do so, you would find someone who *could* run him out!

Or suppose an old hog came into your house and started turning all the furniture upside down and breaking all your lamps and vases. What would you do? You'd run that hog out of your home, wouldn't you? Well, that is also what you'd be inclined to do in the natural if someone came into your house to spoil your goods.

But notice this: Paul said to the Hebrew Christians, "You *took joyfully* the spoiling of your goods." Now, why would those people take joyfully the spoiling of their goods? What if they had said to their adversaries, "Thank God, take all I have! When I get to Heaven, it will be worth it all"? What if they then lived fifty, sixty, or even eighty years after those people had spoiled their goods? Would *you* want to live a long life in which people continually spoiled your goods?

'A Better and an Enduring Substance'

Through the years, religious tradition has taught us to adopt this defeatist attitude: "Just do the best you can down here. One of these days when you get to Heaven, it will be worth all your suffering in this life."

Of course it will be worth all the trials we've gone through when we get to Heaven. But we're not in Heaven right now. Is there anything that makes the Christian life worth living right now while we're still on this earth?

Notice the last part of verse 34: *"...knowing in yourselves that ye have in heaven a better and an enduring substance."* You may have read that verse this way: "Well, when I get to Heaven, I'll have a better and an enduring substance." But that isn't what Paul is saying. He is talking about experiencing a better and an enduring substance right now, *not* when you get to Heaven. Even when someone is trying to spoil your goods, you can enjoy a better and an enduring substance.

Too often we as Christians have been programmed to relegate God's blessings to a future date — to the time when we go to Heaven. We've been taught that the good things of Heaven are of no benefit to us while we are still here on earth.

But that isn't what Paul is saying in this Scripture passage. He is saying that a relationship exists between Heaven and the life a believer lives on this earth right now. He is saying that because

19

the Hebrew Christians were aware of this relationship, they were able to take the spoiling of their goods joyfully. They knew that in Heaven, they had a better and an enduring substance.

Let us consider for a moment what Paul means when he refers to this special "substance." Paul actually refers to this substance again in Philippians 4:19: *"But my God shall supply all your need according to his riches in glory by Christ Jesus."* God supplies our needs not according to our goods, our houses, or our bank accounts, but according to *His riches in glory* by Christ Jesus!

I have taught at various times about *needs* and *desires*. A *need* is something you have to have. But notice what Philippians 4:19 says about the source for meeting your needs. It *doesn't* say the place where you work and are given a paycheck each Friday is your source, does it?

If your job is your source, you are in trouble. I am not saying you should reject your paycheck when your boss hands it to you. But you need to realize that your job is not your source; it is merely the channel through which God is providing your needs. If you place your faith more in your job than in God, you'll be in trouble when the company shuts down and moves somewhere else!

If the Hebrew Christians had placed their faith in their goods, they would have been in great trouble when their goods were spoiled. But they understood that God would meet their needs. *Therefore, the Hebrew Christians took the spoiling of their goods joyfully, knowing that they had a better and an enduring substance in Heaven.*

Those persecuted Christians knew God would meet their needs according that eternal substance, so Paul went on to admonish them, *"Cast not away therefore your confidence, which hath great recompence of reward"* (Heb. 10:35).

You, too, can depend on God to meet your needs according to that better and enduring substance in Heaven. And because you have your needs met according to God's riches in glory by Christ Jesus, God has also instructed you to *cast not away your confidence.*

I have never been as blessed as I am right now in my life, and I am going to continue to be blessed because I will not cast away my confidence. The Bible says my God meets all my needs according to His riches in glory by Christ Jesus. I refuse to cast away my confession of faith in that divine promise, thus making it of no effect in my life.

21

In the face of any need you may face in life, don't cast away your confidence — your confession of faith in the Word of God. In other words, don't cast away what you are saying that is based on God's Word.

The World's System vs. Heaven's System

The Hebrew Christians knew what they were doing. They took the spoiling of their goods with joy, knowing that in Heaven they had a better and an enduring substance and that God supplied their needs according to His riches in glory by Christ Jesus. They understood that God operated with them according to *Heaven's* system, not *the world's* system.

What is the heavenly system like? Well, for one thing, Heaven is paved with streets of gold! Not only that, but the walls are made of jasper and the gates are made of pearl! If God owned all that incredible wealth in Heaven but couldn't send us a loaf of bread, why would we want to trust Him?

Our confidence — what we believe in our hearts and say with our mouths — has great recompense of reward. That word "reward" means *full payment*. When can we enjoy this recompense of full payment? Not when we get to Heaven, but *right now* in this life. No matter what the devil tries to do to spoil our goods, we can claim our great recompense of reward as we refuse to cast away our confidence!

Chapter 3
Patience To Receive the Promise

For ye have need of patience, that, after ye have done the will of God, ye might receive the promise.

Hebrews 10:36

Take a moment to examine your confession in the different arenas of life. You may notice that when you get together with the brethren to rejoice and sing before the Lord, everything coming out of your mouth is top notch and your Word-based confession is flowing.

But what comes out of your mouth when you face the daily situations of life and no one is there to hold your hand or to pray with you? Does your confession remain the same? Are your words based on what God says about the situation? Do you remain patient and steadfast in your confession of faith between the time you pray and the time you receive the actual manifestation of your answer?

When Paul says, "You have need of patience," he is saying, "You need to patiently hold fast to your confidence and keep your confession the same at all times." Why does Paul tell you to do this? He goes on to explain: "So that after you have done the will of God, you might receive the

25

promise — your recompense of reward."

You may say, "Well, God, after You have given me the answer to my prayer, I might believe You. If I could just see You do something, then I would believe."

But that isn't the way it works. God doesn't operate that way. You have need of patience *after* you have done the will of God, and the will of God is that you refuse to cast away your confidence.

If you cast away your confidence, you have not done God's will. Therefore, you must *hold fast* to your confidence. Keep the same confession of faith no matter what circumstances you face, so that after you have done the will of God, you might receive the promise. This is what it means to live by faith.

If You Draw Back, God Has No Pleasure in You

Verse 37 tells us what will happen in the future: *"For yet a little while, and he that shall come will come, and will not tarry."* But in the meantime, verse 38 tells us how to live right now in this life: *"Now the just shall live by faith: but if any man draw back, my soul shall have no pleasure in him."*

The just are to live by faith during their lives on this earth. They do this by not casting away their confidence, or their confession of faith. And if any man draws back and casts away his confession of faith, God says He shall have no pleasure in him.

Do you know that the Bible talks a lot about what you are saying with your mouth? Why is this so? Because God knows that the power of life and death are in your words (Prov. 18:21). That's why Hebrews 10:38 says God will have no pleasure in you if you draw back on your confession of faith. That doesn't mean He won't love you anymore, but it does mean it is impossible to please Him without faith.

Think about what causes you to have pleasure in your children. Suppose you ask your child to do something and he kicks you in the shin and says, "No! I'm not going to do it!" In that case, would you find pleasure in your child? I don't think so. In fact, you would probably engage in the task of giving him the discipline he deserves!

The times you find pleasure in your children are the times they say, "Sure, Dad (or Mom), I'll be glad to do that for you right now," and then they get up and do it. You don't have to say anything else to them; you don't have to remind them over and over again. They just trot right off and do what you asked them to do.

Those are the times you feel like such a proud parent. You tell everyone who will listen to you about the good children you have.

That is what Hebrews 10:38 is telling you. If you draw back from your confession of faith in disobedience to your Heavenly Father's command, He will have no pleasure in you. That doesn't mean God stops loving you, nor does it mean you are lost. It just means you are not affording Him any pleasure.

Your Heavenly Father wants you to give Him pleasure. He wants your fellowship. He wants your love. He wants your communion. But if you are making negative confessions and doing everything contrary to what He has told you to do in His Word, He has no pleasure in you.

Believe Unto The Saving of Your Soul

Paul goes on to say in verse 39, *"But we are not of them who draw back unto perdition; but of them that believe to the saving of the soul."* The word perdition in this verse simply means "lost." Since Paul is talking to saved people here, he is not saying believers are lost if they draw back. He is simply saying they will suffer loss of God's promises.

We find the promises God gave to Abraham and his seed listed in Deuteronomy 28:1-14. We are told that God will bless us coming in and going out. He will bless us in the basket and in the store. He will bless the fruit of our bodies, of our cattle, and the fruit of our ground. All of these are God's promises to Abraham. As Galatians 3:16 says, *"Now to Abraham and his seed were the promises made..."* (Gal. 3:16).

Paul goes on to say in Galatians 3:29, *"And if ye be Christ's, then are ye Abraham's seed, and heirs according to the promise."* What does "the promise" include? For one thing, God promised to bless us in everything we set our hands to do, to prosper us and make us a success in every endeavor we undertake.

Glory! I like success, and I am enjoying it in my life today. It makes no difference whether I am coming in or going out — I am blessed either way, and so are you!

Sad to say, some folks fight for their right to "tribulate." In other words, they insist that God intends for them to suffer through trials of sickness, trouble, and lack in order to teach them something.

If you are fighting for your right to tribulate, just go ahead and tribulate if you want to while I go ahead and get blessed!

You see, I am not one of those who draw back and lose their promises. I am not going to let the devil steal from me. He isn't going to kill and destroy everything good in my life. God has told me not to let the enemy do that. He said, *"Be sober, be vigilant; because your adversary the devil, as a roaring lion, walketh about, seeking whom he may devour: Whom resist stedfast in the faith..."* (1 Peter 5:8,9).

God also said, *"Submit yourselves therefore to God. Resist the devil, and he will flee from you"* (James 4:7). I am going to resist the devil, and he will flee from me. I am going to enjoy the promises of God. I am not going to cast away my confidence. I am not going to draw back unto perdition. I am one of those who believe unto the saving of the soul!

You, too, need to take your place among the just who believe unto the saving of the soul. You see, when you are born again, your soul is not saved. Your *spirit* is the part of you that is saved and now alive unto God.

Your soul is your will, your mind, your emotions, and your intellect. As you do what God tells you to do in His Word, you renew your mind and thus "save" your soul. Addressing fellow believers, Paul talks about this in Romans 12:2: *"And be not conformed to this world: but be ye transformed by the renewing of your mind, that ye may prove what is that good, and acceptable, and perfect, will of God."*

But remember — believing unto the saving of your soul is a process, and during that process you have need of patience. So patiently hold fast to your confidence through every trial and challenge you face. Then after you have done the will of God by persisting in your confession of faith, you *will* receive His precious promises!

Chapter 4
The Rejoicing of the Hope

But Christ as a son over his own house; whose house are we, if we hold fast the confidence and the rejoicing of the hope firm unto the end.

Hebrews 3:6

In Hebrews 3:6, we once again see Paul urging us to *"...HOLD FAST THE CONFIDENCE* the free outspokenness of our confession of faith *and the rejoicing of the hope firm unto the end."* The word *end* here isn't referring to when we get to Heaven. It is talking about fulfillment or completion *within* this life, not about departing *from* this life.

Paul is telling you to hold fast to your confidence unto the *completion* or *fulfillment* of your confession of faith — the words you are speaking about the promises of God coming to pass in your life. Not only are you to hold fast to your confession of faith based on the Word of God, but you are to steadfastly rejoice in hope unto the end — unto the moment of completion when God's promise is actually manifested in the natural realm. You are not to go around talking about all your problems, saying, "When we get through this vale of tears, everything will be all right."

33

Please don't misunderstand — I know that "vale of tears" experiences can happen to believers in this life if they permit them to happen. I am just pointing out a contrast between the two ways Christians can respond to adverse situations in their lives.

For instance, instead of rejoicing in hope unto the end, some Christians say, "I know God put that promise of deliverance in His Word, but He just doesn't understand *my* problem. No one has ever been through what I've been through. I don't even have anyone to talk to about my situation."

If you are honest, you will admit that you've felt like that at some point in your life. But that kind of attitude is wrong. You are to hold fast to your confidence in God's faithfulness. He has promised to meet your needs according to His riches in glory by Christ Jesus!

According to God's Word, we are blessed coming in and going out. The number of our days He has fulfilled because we have set our love upon Him. A thousand shall fall at our side, and ten thousand at our right hand. Only with our eyes shall we behold and see the reward of the wicked. No evil shall befall us, neither shall any plague come near our dwelling (*see* Psalm 91).

However, in order to enjoy all these benefits, we have to fulfill our part of our covenant with God. Our responsibility is simply stated in John 14:15 (author's paraphrase) when Jesus tells His disciples, "If anyone loves Me, he will keep My Word."

So you can see that you can't get the job done by casting away your confidence. You can't even get the job done by maintaining your confession of faith but failing to rejoice in hope.

What did Paul say in Hebrews 10 when those people's goods were destroyed? He said they took it *joyfully*. They understood how the blessings of God were brought to them. They understood how to walk by faith in order to receive the fulfillment of His promises. They understood how to obtain God's best in their lives. In the midst of the spoiling of their goods, they held fast to their confession of faith *with joy* because they knew they had an enduring, everlasting substance in Heaven.

I want to be like those early believers. If all my goods are packed up and taken out of my home, I will still rejoice in God. I know that every time I draw on my supply in Heaven, it does not deplete. The more I draw on it, the more of that "better and enduring" substance there is to meet my needs.

The more I give away, the more I have!

What Is 'the Hope'?

The *hope* Paul is talking about in Hebrews 3:6 simply means *the expected good*. What are you expecting that is good? You should be expecting all of Abraham's promises to be manifested in your life. But first you have to *hold fast* your confidence (your confession of faith), *rejoicing* in the expected good as you *stand firm* unto the end. (In other words, you're not a fireball of faith today and a doubter tomorrow who says, "I don't know if this 'faith stuff' works or not.") As you fulfill your part, those divine promises will become a manifested reality for you.

This holds true for everyone, preachers included. A preacher has to obtain God's promises the same way a layman does. Everyone receives from the Lord *by faith*.

For instance, the Bible says, *"...Let the weak say, I am strong"* (Joel 3:10). It also says, *"...The people that do know their God shall be strong, and do exploits"* (Dan. 11:32). By continually saying what the Word says, the Word comes to life and brings strength to you — *spirit, soul, and body.*

So hold your confidence firm unto the end, or unto the fulfillment of God's promise in your life — until you can see it, hold it, feel it, taste it, and smell it. That's what you have to do if you want to walk in the will of God.

Rejoice *Always*

Philippians 4:4 gives further insight about what it means to rejoice in hope unto the end: *"Rejoice in the Lord alway: and again I say, Rejoice"* (Phil. 4:4). What does rejoicing in the Lord *always* mean? It means you rejoice even in the face of adversity. If people spoil your goods, you continue to rejoice because you know that in Heaven, you have a more enduring substance and that God meets your needs according to His riches in glory by Christ Jesus. Therefore, you can say, "Just let them keep my goods, Lord. I've got so much up in Heaven's storeroom that I will never use it all."

If you ever receive anything from God, you will do it the way He has told you to do it. The just *shall* live by faith. So if you don't receive what is rightfully yours, you have only yourself to blame. By neglecting to live according to your faith in God's Word, you are letting the devil steal from you and destroy what is rightfully yours.

The truth is, a big part of living by faith is learning how to "rejoice in the Lord always." That commandment didn't come from "Charles chapter 4"; it came from Philippians chapter 4, and it is what God has told us to do. I would like to take credit for that divine instruction, but I wasn't around when it was written. However, I will tell you this — *I believe it.*

That verse means you are to rejoice:

- when you get out of the bed every morning.

- when you are on your way to work.

- when the temperature rises to 100 degrees in the shade.

- when your eight-hour protection has broken down.

If you're not rejoicing in the Lord always, you are not in the will of God. If you are not in the will of God, you are not receiving from God. If you are not receiving from God, Satan is robbing you of what is rightfully yours.

Just consider that thought for a moment: Satan is cheating you out of what Jesus went to the Cross to purchase for you — out of what God has said belongs to *you* — if you are not rejoicing in the Lord *always*.

Paul goes on to say in Philippians 4:5, *"Let your moderation be known unto all men. The Lord is at hand."* Paul is saying, "Let your moderation — your willingness not to insist on your own rights with other people — be known unto all men (*not* unto God)."

Some folks absolutely insist on having their own way in their interactions with other people. That is the opposite of what Paul is saying. Christians are to let their moderation be known unto all men. Even if it means they don't get their way with other people all the time, they are still to rejoice.

Why would God tell you to do something like that? He explains at the end of verse 5: *"...the Lord is at hand."* God is right on hand to meet your needs according to His riches in glory by Christ Jesus. So don't insist on your rights from men; rather, *trust God* according to verse 6: *"Be careful for nothing; but in every thing by prayer and supplication with thanksgiving let your requests be made known unto God."* If men cheat you out of something that is rightfully yours, just follow the path of faith and rejoice in the Lord always — and again I say, *rejoice!*

A Negative Confession
Hardens the Heart

God wants us to know His ways, to learn how to move in faith and command the powers of darkness with the Name of Jesus. When we cast away our confidence and maintain a negative confession, that means we do not know the ways of God.

This was the reason the Israelites failed to enter the Promised Land. Hebrews 3:7-12 explains:

Wherefore (as the Holy Ghost saith, Today if ye will hear his voice,

Harden not your hearts, as in the provocation, in the day of temptation in the wilderness:

When your fathers tempted me, proved me, and saw my works forty years.

Wherefore I was grieved with that generation, and said, They do alway err in their heart; and they have not known my ways.

So I sware in my wrath, They shall not enter into my rest.)

Take heed, brethren, lest there be in any of you an evil heart of unbelief, in departing from the living God.

God was grieved with that generation in the wilderness because they did not believe that the Promised Land He had given them was a blessed land, filled with milk and honey.

God had said to them, "I've given this land to you. Everywhere the soles of your feet touch is yours. The enemy is there, but you can go in and drive him out. The land is yours. I have given it to you."

But over and over again, the Israelites said, "We can't take that land — our adversaries are too powerful!" They hardened their hearts with a negative confession. They were simply saying, "We don't care what You say, God. We don't believe You." They didn't know the ways of God; therefore, God was grieved with them and declared, *"...They shall not enter into my rest"* (v. 12).

Let the fate of that generation of Israelites be a warning to you. You also can depart from God with a negative confession. The first time a negative confession comes out of your mouth, you are out of fellowship with God. The relationship has not been broken; you are still His child. *Nevertheless,*

41

doubt breaks fellowship with God, and you have to obtain forgiveness for doubting God in order to restore your fellowship with Him.

Romans 14:23 says, *"And he that doubteth is damned if he eat, because he eateth not of faith: for whatsoever is not of faith is sin."* When we speak things contrary to the Word of God, we are sinning and breaking fellowship with God, and our fellowship isn't restored until we confess our sins to Him. At that moment, He is faithful and just to forgive us our sins and cleanse us from all unrighteousness (1 John 1:9).

Hebrews 3:13 goes on to warn, *"But exhort one another daily, while it is called To day; lest any of you be hardened through the deceitfulness of sin."* Once again, let me stress that a negative confession streaming out of your mouth daily over a period of time will harden your heart to the truth. That negative confession is sin, and it is deceitful. It will cause you to degenerate into a hardened condition in which you can't see the truth. You won't believe truth when it is preached to you; therefore, you will never enter into it.

The Israelites were in that hardened condition when they wandered about in the wilderness for forty years. Only Joshua and Caleb chose to believe God.

Instead of saying, "We can't," these two men confessed their faith: "We *can* do it!" Joshua and Caleb were able to eat of the good of the land because they wouldn't allow their hearts to be hardened through the deceitfulness of sin — in this case, the deceitfulness of a negative confession.

A negative confession will harden your heart until you finally lose all interest and enthusiasm for the things of God and for what God is doing in the earth. On the other hand, you can choose to line up your thinking with God's Word. You can hold fast your confidence and rejoice in hope, standing firm unto the end. You can have patience and keep your confession based on the Word of God.

When you have done these things, you have done the will of God. Consequently, you will be blessed of God — blessed coming in, blessed going out, blessed in the city, blessed in the field, blessed in the basket, blessed in the store, and blessed in the fruit of your body!

'Like a Tree Planted By the Rivers of Water'

Psalm 1:1 says, *"Blessed is the man that walketh not in the counsel* [in words spoken contrary to God's Word, such as a negative

43

confession] *of the ungodly, nor standeth in the way of sinners, nor sitteth in the seat of the scornful."*

How can a believer stand in the way of sinners? By letting a sinner see that he's having a tough time with his Christian life. First the believer complains, "Oh, everything is so bad. I don't know if I'm going to make it. I don't know what's going to happen before the Lord comes." Then he tries to witness to the sinner, "You know, what you need is Jesus. I have Him, and you need Him too!" That sinner is not likely to want Jesus after listening to that Christian complain!

Psalm 2:2,3 goes on to say:

But his delight is in the law of the Lord; and in his law doth he meditate day and night.

And he shall be like a tree planted by the rivers of water, that bringeth forth his fruit in his season; his leaf also shall not wither; and whatsoever he doeth shall prosper.

God says a believer who meditates in the Word of God day and night is like a tree planted by the rivers of water. Why? Because that person is walking in the counsel of God. He is maintaining a confession of faith. He has not cast away his confidence. He confesses continually that his needs are met according to God's riches in glory. He is rejoicing always in the Lord. Therefore, his leaf does not wither. He lives in abundance because *"...whatsoever he doeth shall prosper."*

That's the kind of person you should aspire to be. Align yourself with the Word of God, and hold fast to your confession of faith. Don't cast away your confidence. Hold it firm unto the end as you stand on the Word of God in faith. Rejoice in the Lord always, and again I say, rejoice! Then watch as God begins to work on your behalf so the blessings of Abraham can become a manifested reality in your life!

Chapter 5
Planting Faith Seeds

In an attempt to strengthen their walk of faith, many Christians pray, "Lord, increase my faith." But afterwards, they neither feel anything, hear anything, nor see an angel; therefore, they are confused about whether or not God has answered their prayer.

In truth, God does not increase anyone's faith. A Scripture passage in Luke 17 explains why:

And the apostles said unto the Lord, Increase our faith.

And the Lord said, If ye had faith as a grain of mustard seed, ye might say unto this sycamine tree, Be thou plucked up by the root, and be thou planted in the sea; and it should obey you.

Luke 17:5,6

Apparently, the apostles were having the same problems with feelings of spiritual inadequacy that you and I sometimes have today. So they said to Jesus, "Lord, increase our faith."

But how would the disciples know if Jesus did increase their faith? Would they be able to feel it or

47

see it? Would Jesus set *increased faith* on their front porch in a box? Would they hear bells or see visions? Would they hear an angel saying, "I've come to bring you faith"?

Notice Jesus' interesting response to the disciples' request. In verse 6, He said, *"...If ye had faith as a grain of mustard seed, ye might say unto this sycamine tree, Be thou plucked up by the root, and be thou planted in the sea; and it should obey you."* The apostles wanted Jesus to increase their faith, and He started talking about a grain of mustard seed!

If that happened to us, we might be prone to say, "Lord, I don't want to know about a mustard seed. I want You to increase my faith. What does a mustard seed have to do with increasing my faith?"

Do you believe that Jesus didn't know what He was talking about here? Do you believe that He had "flipped His lid"? Do you believe that He was so scatterbrained that He started talking about something that didn't even relate to what His disciples had asked Him?

No, I'm sure you don't believe that. Apparently, a grain of mustard seed has something to do with increasing our faith. If it doesn't, Jesus wouldn't have answered the way He did.

Referring to this verse, some people say their faith is no bigger than a grain of mustard seed. But Jesus didn't once mention the size of a person's faith in this verse. He said, *"...If ye had faith as a grain of mustard seed...."*

If you had some mustard seeds, what would you do with them? You would *plant* them. So Jesus is telling us, "If you have faith as a grain of mustard seed, *go plant it.*"

Plant Your Faith
By Speaking God's Word

You've probably noticed a certain characteristic of seed when you plant it: It reproduces many of its own kind, multiplying one seed into many seeds. But consider what would happen if you stood in your garden, held your seed in your hand, and said, "I don't believe this seed works, so I'm not going to plant it. It might work for someone else, but it won't work for me." That seed wouldn't reproduce anything. You have to put seed into the ground before it will produce results.

So in His reference to the mustard seed, Jesus was telling the disciples to *plant their faith*. Why did Jesus want to teach His disciples this vital principle? Because He knew that the just shall live by faith and that God has no pleasure in those who draw back from faith.

But how do you go about planting your faith? You do it by *speaking the Word of God.* For instance, you don't say how weak you are. The Word says you are strong, so you plant your faith in that promise by speaking what the Word says about you and calling yourself strong in the Lord.

Jesus illustrated this principle again in Mark 11:23: *"For verily I say unto you, That whosoever shall say unto this mountain, Be thou removed, and be thou cast into the sea; and shall not doubt in his heart, but shall believe that those things which he saith shall come to pass; he shall have whatsoever he saith."* The mountains in your life are the problems that Satan brings against you. Remember, the enemy always comes to steal, kill, and destroy (John 10:10).

You are to speak to those mountains according to God's Word, commanding them to be removed. Your words plant faith in your heart and cause those things you say to come to pass.

Every time you open your mouth to speak forth the Word of God — the *free outspokenness* of your confession of faith — you are planting faith seeds and holding fast to your confidence. And that's just the beginning. When you plant your faith, it inevitably reproduces after its own kind, just as the seed you plant in your garden reproduces after its own kind. For instance, just one kernel of corn could reproduce 100 kernels! Just imagine the enormous harvest you would have if you planted just 200 kernels of corn a day — and then apply that mental picture to your faith walk!

Give Your Faith Seeds
Time To Grow

Do the seeds you plant in your garden only work from 9 to 5 every day and then quit growing until the next day? No, they continue to work 24 hours a day.

Well, seeds of faith do the same. They work while you sleep.

You don't plant seeds in your garden and then come back the next day and say, "I don't understand why I don't see anything sprouting from that seed yet." You know that germination takes several days, so you say, "I know that seed is working. It will soon come up."

Keep that same attitude regarding the faith you've planted in your heart. Don't stop planting seeds of faith. Don't cast away your confidence. The moment you stop planting *seeds of faith*, you will start planting *seeds of doubt and unbelief*. Those seeds of doubt will quickly take root and sprout, choking your faith just as weeds choke your garden and make it less fruitful.

Always remember — faith is planted by what we say and do.

So don't cast away your confidence. Plant faith seeds in your heart with your confession of faith. Guard your heart against doubt, and hold fast to your belief that your words will come to pass. When you do this, God promises that you shall have whatsoever you say!

Faith Is Your Servant

Jesus gave us another important faith principle in Luke 17:7: *"But which of you, having a servant plowing or feeding cattle, will say unto him by and by, when he is come from the field, Go and sit down to meat?"* You may wonder what a servant — someone who waits on you, serves you, or ministers to you — has to do with *faith*. But Jesus was still talking about *faith*; He didn't jump off the subject.

If you had someone working for you and he came to you for instructions, what would you tell him? "Go in the house and take a seat. I'll be right in to wash your feet. I'll also bring you a cold glass of tea and a cool rag to bathe your head, you poor thing, you." No, you wouldn't tell him that. You would tell that servant what you want him to do.

Jesus went on to say verses 8-10:

And will not rather say unto him, Make ready wherewith I may sup, and gird thyself, and serve me, till I have eaten and drunken; and afterward thou shalt eat and drink?

Doth he thank that servant because he did the things that were commanded him? I trow not.

So likewise ye, when ye shall have done all those things which are commanded you, say, We are unprofitable servants: we have done that which was our duty to do.

Jesus is saying that *faith is our servant* and that *faith has a duty to fulfill.* God has instructed us to cast the mountain (our problems, cares, troubles, and anything else the enemy throws at us) into the ocean. As we obey that divine command, our servant, faith, will do what we tell him to do.

Tell Your Faith What To Do

When your servant finishes the task you tell him to do, he won't do anything else until you tell him to. In the same way, your servant, faith, will only work by the confession of your mouth that is based on the Word of God. Faith will continue to work according to your confession until it pushes that mountain into the ocean. As long as you allow faith to push your mountains, it will keep on pushing.

But if you say, "Hey, faith, come on home," faith will obey you; it will quit pushing and come on home. It won't ask questions. It won't argue with you. It won't say anything back to you. That mountain may be just one-quarter inch from the sea. But if you call your faith back in, it will quit working, and the mountain of problems will remain standing in your life.

That's why you have to determine, "I am not one of those who call their faith home. I am not one of those who draw back unto perdition and lose the promise. I am one of those who believe unto the saving of the soul and the renewing of the mind! I speak only according to God's Word, and my faith obeys my words to bring God's promises to pass in my life!"

Chapter 6
Partakers of Christ

Many people believe that once they are born again, God's blessings come to them automatically from then on. But that isn't true. Hebrews 3:14 says, *"For we are made partakers of Christ, IF we hold the beginning of our confidence in other words, if we hold fast our confession of faith in the Word of God stedfast unto the end."*

A partaker is a *partner*. If we are made partakers, or partners, of Jesus, we are made partakers of joy, peace, happiness, longsuffering, patience, health, soundness, healing, deliverance, and safety. But if we don't hold fast to our confession of faith, we are not made partakers of all those divine blessings.

Suppose there was one person who had a testimony of a great healing and another person who had maintained his confession of faith all through his life and lived or walked in divine health. Which person do you think everyone would be more likely to listen to?

Actually, the one who walks in divine health has the greater testimony of the two. Praise God for that person who received his healing! But at the same time, the person who has lived in divine health all his life knows something about living in faith that I want to hear. I should be able to learn something valuable from that individual that can help me in my own walk of faith.

A Partaker of All That God Is

Second Peter 1:4 says that *I am made a partaker of the divine nature*. I am made a *partaker* of all that God is. I am made a partaker of *His power*. I am made a partaker of *His glory*. I am made a partaker of *His riches in glory*. God said that I am made a partaker of all these covenant benefits *if* I hold the beginning of my confidence *steadfast unto the end*.

I have seen people start off with good intentions and a confession of faith. But as the days come and go, Satan's persistent efforts to discourage them begin to take effect.

Obstacles and problems begin to make these people feel weary, and they start to cast away their confidence. Thus, they get themselves into a situation where they are wavering back and forth between faith and doubt. Today they have a good confession of faith. When tomorrow comes with different circumstances and situations, their confession becomes negative. The Bible warns, "Let not that man think he will receive *anything* from God" (see James 1:6-8).

Confidence: The Foundation

Let's look at Hebrews 3:14 again: *"For we are made partakers of Christ, if we hold the beginning of our confidence stedfast unto the end"* (Heb. 3:14). The word *confidence* in this verse of Scripture is a different Greek word than the one used in Hebrews 10:35. Here, *confidence* means "foundation."

When we first believe God for a specific petition, we *lay a foundation of faith* by planting faith seeds with the free outspokenness of our confession of God's promises. Then we must hold the beginning of our foundation *"...stedfast unto the end"* (or unto the fulfillment of what we are believing for) so our planted faith seeds have the opportunity to sprout and grow. As we hold our *confidence* steadfast until our faith has caused our petition to become visible in the physical realm, we are made *partakers with Christ* — partakers of His health, His grace, His glory, of everything that He is.

The Danger of Speaking Contrary to God's Word

Remember, you sow seeds of faith for everything that God has provided for you by *saying what God says in His Word.* Now consider that truth in light of Hebrews 3:15: *"While it is said, To day if ye will hear his voice, harden not your hearts, as in the provocation* [the time the Israelites rebelled against the Lord in the wilderness]" (Heb. 3:15). Paul is urging Christians not to harden their hearts by casting away their confidence, speaking negative confessions of doubt and unbelief — everything but the Word of God.

As we've seen, the deceitfulness of sin will harden a person's heart. That's what happened to the Israelites, and the consequences were devastating: *"For who, having heard, rebelled? Indeed, was it not all who came out of Egypt, led by Moses? Now with whom was He angry forty years? Was it not with those who sinned, whose corpses fell in the wilderness?"* (vv. 16,17).

The Israelites sinned with a negative confession. They went about confessing that they didn't believe what God said. They said, "We can't do it. We're not big enough. The giants are too big, and we are as grasshoppers in our own sight" (Num.

58

13:33). They said everything but the Word of God, and God labeled this as *sin*.

Paul is exhorting you to avoid sinning as the Israelites did by determining to always speak in line with the Word of God. Hold fast to your confession of faith. Hold fast to what God has said to you through His Word, and don't let it go. Hang on to it until the fulfillment of it has come to pass.

Verse 18 goes on to say, *"And to whom sware he that they should not enter into his rest, but to them that believed not?"* How did the Israelites "believe not"? By saying, "We can't do it, Lord. I know You said it, but You don't understand our situation. Lord, this is impossible."

Perhaps you have prayed this type of prayer at some point in your life: "Lord, I don't understand it. Why did You tell me to do something that is so hard to do? Lord, if I could just know for sure. If You would just let me hear some bells ring in the morning at three o'clock, I'd know it is You. Lord, if I could just see a blue light streaking out of Heaven at one thirty in the morning, *then* I would believe."

No, you wouldn't! You would just exclaim, "What in the world is that?" and be no further along in your faith walk than you were before!

You see, if you won't believe the Word of God, you wouldn't believe blue lights or bells tinkling in the middle of the night. You wouldn't even believe an angel if one walked into your bedroom and told you, "I have a message from God"!

Verse 19 tells us what happens when people cast away their confidence, or their confession of faith: *"So we see that they could not enter in* [the Promised Land, which was a land of rest] *because of unbelief."*

The Promised Land is a type of Kingdom living here on this earth, not when we get to Heaven. How do I know that? God told the children of Israel to go into the land and *drive out the giants* (the inhabitants). Well, we won't have any "giants" to drive out of our lives once we reach Heaven. It is only in this earthly life that we have to overcome the enemy that seeks to steal, kill, and destroy!

Hold Fast!

So hold fast to your confession of faith, using the sword of the Spirit — the Word of God — to defeat Satan at every turn. Enter into your promised land of divine blessings, and drive the enemy out of there! As you do, you will experience what it means to be made a partaker of Christ, for every need you could ever have is already met according to God's riches in glory by Christ Jesus.

Take time to get God's Word down into your heart. Meditate on it. Read it. Study it. *Plant* the Word of God in your heart; then speak the Word with your mouth. *If* you hold fast the beginning of your confidence — your foundation of faith in God's Word — steadfast unto the end, you are made a partaker with Jesus of Nazareth. Praise God! That's good news! As a partaker, you can claim Jesus' incredible promise in Mark 11:24: *"...What things soever ye desire, when ye pray, believe that ye receive them, and ye SHALL have them."*

Don't forget First John 5:14,15, which guides you further along the way to becoming a partaker of God's benefits: *"And this is the confidence* [the free outspokenness of our confession of faith] *that we have in him, that, if we ask any thing according to his will, he heareth us: And if we know that he hear us, whatsoever we ask, we know that we have the petitions that we desired of him."*

You must ask according to God's will. His will is in His Word. You know He hears you because you pray according to His will — His Word.

Therefore, you know you have whatsoever petition that you desire. This is what it means to move in confidence.

If you are not moving in confidence, then you don't yet have your foundation built to receive from God and to be made a partaker of Christ. But when *you know that you know* that you know that you have asked in line with His Word, which is His will, you can tell everyone that you already have your answer. God and all His angels in Heaven are bound by His Word to bring it to pass for you!

So no matter what problems, obstacles, or adverse circumstances come your way, *hold fast*! *Don't cast away your confidence!* Remember, God says that your confidence has great recompense of reward in this life — no less than *payment in full!*

Prayer of Salvation

Confidence to receive God's blessings begins with Jesus. The Bible says that Jesus came to give you an abundant, healthy, whole, prosperous life. This all begins by receiving Jesus as your Savior and Lord and then allowing Him to lead and guide you every day in all that you say and do.

If you have never done this and are ready to take this step into God's family right now, please pray the following prayer from your heart:

Dear Heavenly Father,

I come to You in the Name of Jesus. I know I have sinned and fallen short of Your glory. I know You love me and gave Your Son Jesus to be crucified for my sin.

The Bible says in Romans 10:9, *"...If thou shalt confess with thy mouth the Lord Jesus, and shalt believe in thine heart that God hath raised him from the dead, thou shalt be saved."* I believe that Jesus Christ is the Son of God. I believe He died on a Cross for my sin, was buried, and then rose again. I now commit myself to Jesus, making Him the Lord of my life.

Thank You, Father, that I am born again and that I am now Your child. My eternity will be spent with You in Heaven! In Jesus' Name, amen.

If you prayed this prayer for the first time, please let me know by writing to the address listed on the following page. I'd like to send you free material to help you get started in your new life in Christ.

For Further Information

For additional copies of this book
and other books, audiotapes, and videotapes,
please visit our on-line bookstore at
www.victoriousliving.org.

For further information
regarding Charles Cowan's ministry
schedule please write or call:

Faith Is the Victory Church

P. O. Box 160268

3344 Walton Lane

Nashville, Tennessee 37216

1-800-842-7896

E-mail: victoriousliving@aol.com

About the Author

Charles Cowan was born and raised a pastor's son in a small town in Kentucky. It was in that small town that he first sensed the call of God on his life. It was also there that he met and married Sue, his wife of more than  forty years. Charles and Sue have six children.

Because of the divine call on his life, Charles moved his family to Tulsa, Oklahoma, in 1974 to attend Rhema Bible Training Center. Upon his graduation, he started a Bible study in Nashville, Tennessee. The Bible study grew and became what is now Faith Is The Victory Church, with a thriving congregation of more than 1,400 people.

In his ministry of more than thirty-five years, Charles Cowan has been privileged to minister the Word of God in more than twelve nations of the world. He has taught in various churches in twenty-six states, in addition to fulfilling his role as pastor to a growing congregation. Charles has a deep desire to see people apply the Word of God to their lives so it can transform them into what God has made them to be. *It's all about Jesus.* That's the message that flows from the heart of Charles Cowan.